Cinderella

Cinderella was a young girl who lived
with her wicked stepmother and two
ugly stepsisters.

One day a messenger came to the house with an invitation to a ball at the palace.
The stepsisters were very excited.
"We must make ourselves look beautiful for the handsome prince," they said..
"Can I come to the ball?" asked Cinderella.
"You?" the ugly stepsisters laughed.
"Of course you can't," snapped the stepmother.
"You have to stay here and do the housework!"

Soon the big day arrived. Cinderella spent the day helping her stepsisters get ready for the ball. "Wash my hair! Find my necklace!" they shouted.

"The prince will dance with me first because my dress is more beautiful than yours," said one stepsister.

"Rubbish," said the other. "My hairstyle is far prettier than yours!"

Finally, Cinderella's stepmother and stepsisters were ready to go to the ball. They left without even saying goodbye to poor Cinderella.

Cinderella was very sad. She really wanted to go to the ball and see the prince. She sat down and cried.
"I wish I could go to the ball but I don't have any beautiful clothes to wear," she said to herself.

Suddenly, Cinderella heard a voice. It was
a kind voice. Cinderella looked up and saw
an old lady.
"Cinderella," she said. "I'm your fairy godmother.
Don't cry. You shall go to the ball!"

"But how is that possible?" asked Cinderella.
"I don't have a ball gown."
"Do as I say and you will go to the ball,"
replied the fairy godmother, smiling.
The fairy godmother told Cinderella to fetch a
pumpkin from the garden. The fairy godmother
touched the pumpkin gently with her magic
wand and it turned into a beautiful carriage.
Then she touched Cinderella's rags with her
magic wand and transformed them into
a beautiful pink ball gown and
her shoes into sparkling glass
slippers.

"Oh, thank you so much, Fairy Godmother!" cried Cinderella. "Now, off you go to the ball," said the fairy godmother, "but remember, you must leave before midnight or your beautiful gown will turn back into rags."

When Cinderella arrived at the palace, everyone turned to admire the mysterious princess.
When the prince saw Cinderella, he instantly fell in love with her.
"Who's that beautiful princess?" he asked, but no one knew.

"She is the most beautiful guest at the ball!" everyone exclaimed in amazement.
The handsome prince danced with Cinderella all evening. He hardly noticed any of the other guests. Cinderella's ugly stepsisters were very jealous of the mysterious princess.

Cinderella was having such a wonderful evening that she didn't notice the time until she heard the clock striking twelve. Suddenly, she remembered her fairy godmother's warning. "I have to go now!" she exclaimed, running down the steps of the palace.

"Wait!" cried the prince, but Cinderella was gone. Cinderella ran so quickly that she left one of her tiny glass slippers behind.
By the stroke of midnight everything returned to normal and Cinderella ran home in her ragged clothes. The prince found the glass slipper on the step. He sat down on his chair in the palace.
"I will marry the girl whose foot fits this slipper," he decided.

The next day the prince ordered the royal messenger to visit every house in the land and ask each girl to try on the glass slipper.
The messenger arrived at Cinderella's house. "The prince will marry the owner of this glass slipper!" he announced. The two ugly stepsisters tried and tried but they could not squeeze their huge feet into the dainty slipper.
The messenger was about to leave when Cinderella came into the room.

"Please may I try the slipper?" she asked the messenger shyly.

"You?" screamed Cinderella's stepmother. "You're just a servant girl!"

Cinderella's stepmother and ugly stepsisters complained and stamped their feet but the messenger invited Cinderella to sit down. He put the slipper on her foot and it fitted perfectly! Cinderella took the other slipper out of her pocket. The ugly stepsisters were horrified! How could scruffy Cinderella be the mysterious, beautiful princess?

Cinderella was taken to the palace and a few days later, the palace held the largest and most beautiful wedding anyone had ever seen. Everyone in the kingdom was invited, including Cinderella's ugly stepsisters.

So, Cinderella and her handsome prince were married and they lived happily ever after.